Swallowing the Light

Swallowing the Light

Poems by

John Schneider

Cover design by Shay Culligan
Cover photo by Peter Schneider

ISBN: 978-1-63980-188-6

Kelsay Books
502 South 1040 East, A-119
American Fork, Utah 84003
Kelsaybooks.com

For Donna

Acknowledgments

The American Journal of Poetry: "Looking for the House with the Body"
Anak Sastra: "Vibul"
Atticus Review: "Eight Points"
The Bitter Oleander Press: "Communal Oven"
The Bookends Review: "Wolf at the Door"
California Fire and Water: A Climate Crisis Anthology: "When 'If' Turns to 'When'"
California Quarterly: "Off the Dock," "A Second Look," "Reading Our Limbed Monterey Pine"
Canary: "Sea Lion"
fort da: "Cultivation"
The Inflectionist Review: "Myanmar Monk," "Puzzle Pieces"
The Literary Nest: "Lament," "Beyond the Field"
Lullwater Review: "The Scent of Citrus"
Mason Street: "Oasis," "Temple Dogs"
Neologism Poetry Journal: "Cuttings, Mid-September Morning"
North Dakota Quarterly: "Two Nights Under Rough Wool"
The Orchards Poetry Journal: "Cathedral"
Poetica Review: "Missing My Daughter"
The Potomac Review: "Singer"
Slipstream Poetry Magazine: "Cadaver Lab," "If the Ants Stop Moving, If the Flies Don't Land"
Tampa Review: "Bottomless Water"
West Trade Review: "My Father's Last Year"
The Worcester Review: "Mississippi," and "Mother Poems"

Special thanks to *Atlanta Review* for selecting "Black Sand Beaches" as a Merit Award Winner in their 2021 International Poetry Contest.

Also, special thanks to *Slipstream Poetry Magazine* for nominating "Cadaver Lab" and to *The Orchards Poetry Journal* for nominating "Cathedral" for the Pushcart Prize.

Also by John Schneider

Non-Fiction

Dreaming and Being Dreamt: The Psychoanalytic Function of Dreams

Contents

The Noises of Night

" . . . one must cast a beam of intense darkness so that something that has hitherto been observed by the glare of the illumination can glitter all the more in the darkness."

—Lou Andres-Salome

¤

Interlopers

¤

Bleached skeletons of fish
like leafless tree trunks in autumn—
our insides revealed

In the Medina of Fes

Teacup hooves clatter
on cobbled pavement.

     Donkeys flow

through these narrow
alleyways, legs

delicate yet steady,

     in sync

with nodding heads.
Some carry brown

propane tanks
into the village

     while others

haul out canvas bags
brimming with waste.

A man hollers,

     "Balak, Balak"
     —make way
     make way.

Leather halter in hand,
he leads his donkeys,

     their shoulders burdened

with flat screen TV's
secured in a jumble
of plastic twine.

For a moment the screens

       fill with sunlight—

slow-motion broadcasts
bustling people
in hooded jabalas.

The beasts' leathery odor
mixes with the aroma of spices

       and settles

in the still air between
cavernous dun-colored buildings.

On the rooftops above,
ten thousand
internet dishes

       rise to face Mecca.

Myanmar Monk

—The Saffron Revolution, 2007

After the soldiers murdered the monks, he told me
in his best English over his best tea,

they cremated the wounded and the dead
together in mass graves.

Swollen lips still moaning as the ovens shut.
Then the soldiers snuck off to the monastery

to give alms to the remaining monks.
Expecting forgiveness. Like us all.

When half the monks refused
to turn over their lacquered bowls,

the soldiers returned after dark:
hauling sleepy monks from their sanctuaries,

dousing them with insect spray,
firing wildly into their final screams.

The wounded scaled walls barefoot, leaving
bloody footprints halfway to heaven.

Temple Dogs

* *November 17, 1997*

Ayman Told Me

it was on his birthday:
six men laughing and singing,
posing as tourists at Luxor's finest funerary temple
shot the cashier and guards then opened fire.
Bullets ricocheted off red-granite columns
foreign families cowered, ran

slipping on spilled blood, hunted like dogs,
the dead and dying mutilated for spite.
Others feigning death, crumpled
bodies like litter on limestone floors.

Sixty-three tourists. And the killers fled
past checkpoints to a cave in the mountains.
That afternoon, their corpses lay in the city square,
dumped like garbage on the unswept sandstone.

Adults and children crying, jeering,
spitting into their open mouths.
In the temple—silence.
A single police car's red light
flashing until dawn.

** *The Next Day*

Ayman Told Me

he went to the temple, rubbed his fingers
over the cartouche peppered with holes,

heard the bristles scrubbing death off the floor,
smelled the acrid air, sacrificial blood
still staining the pink limestone.

Witnessed a Coptic priest tossing holy water,
crossing himself, kissing a crucifix,
burning incense to release trapped spirits.
Overheard a Muslim cleric chanting from the Koran,
muttering verses to honor wandering souls.
Was blessed by two holy men crisscrossing grim paths

while unshaven guards leaned against columns,
yellow-stained fingers holding still smoldering cigarettes.

*** *Years Later*

Ayman Told Me

to expect nothing, no sign at all,
no plaque, memorial, no special security,
only recumbent sphinxes circling the door.

He said Egyptians believe it is better to forget
the horror: bleached, dried, blasted by sands
back into the endless desert.

In the temple, a pack of dogs, brittle
mangy pariahs the color of scabs,
lurk in the holy shadows, staring
with wary eyes, no barking, growling,
just panting like us all for air.

Maasai Mara

By day's end, clusters of wildlife watch
the kicked-up dust mingle with wildebeest
bleats and the deafening buzz of cicadas.

Stands of acacia, their leaves drying to parchment,
surround rivulets stilled by summer heat.

::

Then, the next morning, another story begins.

::

Bits of bone, scraps of fur—scattered over
ground stained brown from smeared feces—
blood-coated grass, and a bloody-faced lion.

The stragglers, the weak, the lame, those out
of step will be culled from the herd.

Interloper

At first light on the Serengeti
I came upon a cheetah
exhausted from the night's hunt,
red-faced, whiskers dripping blood—

stooping to shit—wholly alert,
its ears attuned to danger.
Still my hands moved quickly
to cover my eyes, offering
privacy, a human gesture.

::

Years later, on my morning run in Tilden Park,
I came upon a coyote feeding on
the hindquarters of a freshly downed doe—

not a familiar scene so close to home
where deer bed down beneath blackberry brambles
before morning light warms the fog away.

I imagined the terror of the doe,
her panic-stricken heart,
the dead silence after.

Witnessing a predator tear
and swallow entrails, undisturbed
until his eyes met mine upslope,
it was no longer clear which one of us
had been caught.

Through a Gap in the Thicket

Beyond the nettle bushes the two of them stood
nose to nose, each staring into the other's eyes
not concerned that I was watching,

antlers locked together. Earth shaking.
And that brutal calm between each collision.

When it was over, one ram strode away,
almost tranquilly, with its bloody ornaments,
the air heavy with baked dung and musk.

The other stepped gracefully through a gap
in the Tanzanian thicket to a waiting ewe
patient, statuesque, anticipating the chance

of child. The dappled light bounced off her
fur, luminous, a sheen you might see
on pristine porcelain figurines.

What We Know

After the storm, curls of ochre carpet the road.
Shorn from the blue gum eucalyptus,

their imprint on the wet macadam—
exquisite batik patterns.
Before the bark curls into scroll, it twists

towards the warming sun in a swirl of wind.
Above our heads speckled light filters through.
Our world familiar again.

Green once more, the hills stretch
softly like cupped hands
cradling the landscape.

Red-tailed hawks halo
the treetops, grasslands, then back.
As if watching over us.

In West Sumatra I once witnessed peasants,
gentle mannered as a windless morning
outside sun-streaked Bukkittinghi.

They spread armfuls of cinnamon rind
on orange and red batik cloths to dry in the sun
on strips of hardpack between homes.

From their corrugated tin porches, families
oversee the harvest, nodding their approval.

The fragrance of freshly peeled trees
stayed with me, a story I sometimes tell
my children, who now take their turn
playfully gathering *cinnamon* by the handful
for hot-buttered toast with sugar.

In the High Atlas Mountains of Morocco

We stopped at a wayside café for sugary mint tea. Behind
      the mudbrick building stained by Hookah smoke, two
puppies lolled in the sun on that chilly October afternoon:
      one bouncing about, curiously
nuzzling the other to play—
      listless and disoriented,
his ribs showing, glazed eyes pale,
      a commotion of flies swarming it.
The cook stepped through the rear screen door
      for a cigarette break, a thin man with a heavy beard
wearing a Boston Bruins baseball cap
      nodding as he said *ssalamu lekum.*
We asked him about the strays—
      Berber mountain dogs
common to the area for centuries,
      their mother killed by a lorry on the highway.
The second seems sick, we observed.
      He picked up the puppy, moving it
like a ragdoll to prove it still had some life.
      Is there a hospital or vet in the area?
No,
      here we have no hospitals, he apologized.
For animals or our children.
      And I am sorry about Las Vegas, so many dead.

If the Ants Stop Moving, If the Flies Don't Land

I once sat in a beach hut in Papeete
nursing a can of Hinano, and listened to tales
told and retold by four island fishermen—
their chocolate-brown eyes gone sea-flecked gray—
about the dangers of eating coral reef fish.

::

Polynesian children hold for life
the lessons passed by the elders
on how to tell if the brightly colored-
fish they catch and eat daily
contain ciguatera toxins:

Cut the heads off and wait for enough blood
to drain to attract red and black ants
and tropical flies. Allow the ants to crawl
onto the fish; if the ants stop moving,
if the flies don't land, don't eat: the fish will kill you.

::

If I wanted to die, I would find a more efficient way
than eating coral reef fish. But I don't want to die.

I want to flick away death like an ant off my leg,
for all this healthy eating, exercise, sleep to mean something.

For all my travels to have taught me one thing
that keeps death at bay. To be less vulnerable.

To be more than just another story told and retold
and eventually forgotten.

Vibul

He was the lucky one smiling
as we shivered outside
the jungle ruins
on the paths of Angkor Wat
in driving August rains.

He was the lucky one born
of peasant farmers,
common laborers
tilling Pol Pot's soil—
not of the New People.

No need to feign allegiance.
No need to hide
books inside pockets.
No thoughts to suppress
or dreams to erase.
No education but in suffering.

Born on some day
his mother could not recall
while Nixon emptied bombs
from the belly of a B52
near the Ho Chi Minh Trail.

She holds her own belly.
He bulges to be born.
Bombs drown her screams,
hiding in the *family hole*
deep below the rice paddy.

Hungry children wail,
penned in bamboo huts,
necks craned through slats,
as mothers slave dawn to dusk
for a cup of *babaw*.

Filling his pockets
with crickets and bugs
and a frog to roast,

he was the lucky one who stood
in terror while others marched by
to be killed by the Khmer Rouge,
their organs eaten by soldiers.

Machine guns growl.
Rain turns the paddy red.
Leeches swim in the blood.
Farmers chase dogs gnawing human
bones to be burned at the monastery.

Vibul was the lucky one fleeing
through fields where brown cows
huddled, nostrils flared, staring
at bloated bodies buzzing with flies.

He is the happy-go-lucky one,
who got to pick his own birthday.
"Make me two years older, please.
Easy to remember; helps to forget."

Misremembered light
ghosts carry sweet shame—
tainted nostalgia

Two Nights Under Rough Wool

In my brother's barracks
two teenage protesters
sleep in the empty bunks
of soldiers gone to Nam.

That night, under cheap Army
blankets again, my friend and I
play war with a dog-eared deck
of old cards missing all its kings
while my older brother is off
drinking with men who haven't
yet lost themselves.

::

As kids, we slept under the same
blankets—coarse, cheap, moth-proof—
until returning one day from school
to find matching store-bought spreads
quilted in greens and rust and gold.

But no mother—gone for surgery again.
No longer worried about her canning jars
filled with silver anniversary dollars.
No longer saving them for a worthy cause.

No longer fearing one son's war
and how the other will one day fill
his empty bunk under the same rough wool.

Communal Oven

In Marrakech, round the corner from a stylish Riad in the medina I come upon a communal oven just inside an arched doorway, where battered metal racks hold rounds of just-baked bread and sesame cookies covered with damask towels. Inside, the darkness fills with the fragrance of argan and awe and the flickering light from olive branches burns in the *faraan*. The baker, his upper body visible above the brick oven, pilots his long-handled wooden paddle into this cave, sliding loaves in and out, repositioning them to satisfy each household's taste. Local women drive up on scooters or send children to drop off bread dough kneaded and divided into rounds covered with an old kitchen towel.

Then the women are gone, no discussions no greetings each towel pattern a signature of its owner, some checked in blue, some white gone to gray, so the baker can return the perfect baked loaf to each family.

I wonder about the boys moving with purpose through these streets—six- or seven-year-olds—carrying wooden platters with sticky bread dough rounds, looking solemn as altar boys delivering communion bread and wine to the priest during mass, for the congregation to be made one in spirit. In Morocco, bread replaces forks when families join to eat communally, taking bites from the same bowl, creating *Baraka,* a spiritual energy flowing from the bread maker to each family.

Talking in Myanmar

—At the Temple of the Golden Buddha

In one hand he carries a bamboo cage
holding a tiny sparrow.

With the other he gestures
as if talking about the golden Buddha
but instead confides to me:

> *I former teacher*
> *they see me*

> *in demonstration photo*
> *take away rights*

> *In Rangoon*
> *I in jail, in local police station*

> *two, three nights*
> *police say don't do anymore that*

> *What do? Nothing*
> *walking, planting,*

> *now sixteen years moved here*
> *I teach in evening*

> *young children 10–12, happy*
> *I love to teach free.*

He lifts the top of the cage
to release the sparrow.

It does not fly
until he blows on it.

Not a Muslim

We can feel the fine Sahara dust
against our faces as we move through
the old Arab quarter of Casablanca.

Sounds of the medina color everything:
business conducted in high pitched
abbreviations, thrumming mandolin strings
from a room above the *souq,*

the sound of a heavy mallet's thump as it
halves goat heads the butcher
positions on a table,

blood still spurting
their bulging jellied eyes savored
by honored guests during Eid Al-Adhal—

the festival celebrating
Abraham's willingness to kill his son.
Everywhere the plaintive bleats of sheep.

A woman comes forward to haggle
with the butcher. Her voice rises and falls
as she negotiates.

I hear about the shooting back home
when we stop for mint tea. *Thank God,*

he's not a Muslim, says Ahmed about the shooter,
his hands gesturing in circles. *Every time it's bad,*
they say another Muslim! He gestures again.

When they find out he's not Muslim, they say
it's only an accident.

You're right, I say 62
dead is never an accident.

Silently we watch a peddler enter the medina
through its keyhole-shaped arch, olive switch in hand.

Oasis

Crossing Jordan from Amman through Karak to Wadi Rum
I snake over endless hills of silent gunpowder
spiraling up, twisting down molten macadam.
One-humped camels bob along the blue where sky meets sand.

My caravan of one passes Bedouin camps. Resting camels shield
their eyes with a third lid, nosing empty gas cans for a drink.
Time passes unpursued while life shrinks from the merciless day.
In late August, you cannot stand so deep in afternoon's shadows.

The heat seeps into boot soles, smolders into bones, boiling
marrow. White with stubble, my face ghosts with sweat.
Dried saliva seals my mouth. My mind sears with
half-forgotten picture-book images of

Lot's wife turning to a pillar of salt,
Jesus' baptism in the River Jordan
by a man in goat hides eating locusts and wild honey.
Cicadas burrow deep into sand where even faith cannot reach.

::

There are no sounds beyond the static murmur of the Dead Sea.
Somewhere between Amman and Petra, I pull into a village's
sole hotel, its chipped stucco walls holding tight the sun.

In my room, slumped in a chair, red
with exhaustion, I order lentil soup
brought to me by a beardless man.

Eat before it gets cold, he tells me.
Squeeze lemon. Good for heat. You from U.S.?
I was in American Camp D-2. Afghanistan.
Food service for Jordanian company.

When I back to Amman, bowed
on all fours, kissed the ground.

Home.

He leaves me to my soup.

The days stupor breaking, sand no longer
hissing. In the plaza below, human shadows
begin to appear in doorways. Mouths move
around unfinished conversations.

The phone trills, *How was soup?*
I come for tray? A gentle knock.

                              So, what happened in Afghanistan?

He turns away.

Taliban soldiers shoot bullets in air.
Know they'll come down on American mess tent.
Saw many Americans die that day.

One guy chopping onions on cutting board.-
He leans forward, bullet hits him in head.
Bullets falling through tent. Men crawling
like fish on bellies beneath tables.

Bloody bodies beside pots and pans
Yelling, moaning, thuds, then only
faucet running, oil cans, bodies, spurting.

Why would you leave your home for that?

My heart.

::

A broken heart?

Raised together, from this age (his hand leveled
halfway up his thigh) to age 15, she move
from Petra to Amman. I writing her.
Parents break it off, refuse calls, hide my letters.
Marry her off to someone else.

There been no one else since.
One never forgets someone so special.

Like moon and stars in sky and rivers running through forest.

He turns to go.
I hold out money,

no, no. I thank you for hearing me.

41

¤

Last Season's Decay

¤

Autumn's dimming light
time to reflect on our ghosts—
days shorten, frail, falling

Bearings

Guidebooks instruct us
to look for fixed points
along the trail.

To take advice from
centuries-old pines
logging time beside
monumental boulders
and peaks that pierce
the bluest sky.

Yet a trail can become
obscured—in fog, rain,
sleet, snow, darkness—
our cardinal directions lost.

We need our own True North,
not found in guidebooks,
mostly invisible
absorbed early on from our compass rose:
what we turn toward.

How we might one day learn
to find our way back.

As If to Be Invisible

At first, it seemed   a robin's nest
rounded bark fiber   so exact
woven loom-   tight and sealed
with a porcelain-like   veneer

until I noticed the sleek   grey fur,
impossibly red eyes,   its wild
handiwork shaped into   such a fine
container for its young   beneath
the nearby redwood pile:

a roof rat, stealing   away on tiptoe,
shrinking into itself as if   to be invisible,

almost debonair, nonchalant,   refined,
prancing away as if I   couldn't see
the difference,   as if there is no
                              difference between

It Was the Freedom of Blue Light

—Art is the lie to help us see the truth, Pablo Picasso

It was how the morning sun
tinted the emerald lake-top and winter-blue sky.

It was something more than a sunrise.
The predawn light rose like vapor off the lake,

its warm blue entering the morning
dissolving the snow off Sierra granite

brightening red-twig-dogwood branches
and me becoming the color blue

barren of concerns.
It was the freedom of blue light

staring back, a message from the other side
demanding nothing

my role just to let the inner blue of snow pass through
me with the evenness of winter birdsong,

the way Picasso's *Old Guitarist* was freed
to become the blue behind him

his sightless elongated brown body
blending with the background, translucent.

Mayfly

its iridescence dazzles yellow
      as the fly line sweeps
the sky curling
        loop after loop
the suspended monofilament
          buzzes through the air
between the deep river below
           and deeper cerulean sky
inviting the dry fly to join the cloud of insects
          it imitates
controlled by a flick of the wrist it lands
        in just the right place
the way our dreams are twined
      to what we've left unresolved
yet float freely to the surface
      to be mostly forgotten
flickering in and out of awareness
    as they fill the emptiness
between silent sky and deeply unsilent river

Off the Dock

We had fished from that dock since we were children
always between daylight and dark, always
surface casting as far as possible, sending

the lure carried by its own weight,
the line from the reel unspooling
with ease, between the flattened bottom of the sky

and the shimmering top of the lake
to hook browns, rainbows, and cutthroats.
One night, we flashed a light into the water

at our feet, illuminating a spot
about as large as arms spread into embrace.
Below us, fish of all sizes

and shapes going about their business:
crawdads pursuing minnows,
minnows chasing sculpins and mysis shrimp.

That it took so many years to notice
what had always been there, still hurts.

Black Sand Beaches

Shorebirds scurry back and forth across the beach,
their thousand legs wound beneath stoic bodies
moving on pencil-thin feet, leaving
hieroglyphics on the sand. Then they scatter,

chasing the bristling surf out, then turning
to make a three-toed retreat, escaping
the froth of waves, darting just beyond
reach of the sea's foaming tongue. I have

watched them blown by blustery seas and spindrift
until evening light gives way to darkness.
Later, I lie in bed, washed over by moonlight
drifting in and out of sleep.

Images that grieve me come and go, characters
crisscross my mind, then slip out of reach, while
standing arabesque, one eye open, somewhere
shorebirds sleep on black-sand beaches.

Decoy

Rising from   the sedges, ducks
gather in dim morning   light
for another   shared migration—

    a life's work—

a semblance   of wooden effigies
perfectly painted   in natures' hues
luring them closer   within range

    inevitably toppling

in the northerly wind   as a blur
of feathers and family   cut open
the clouds   the sky   unwounded

Self-Portrait Without an Inch of Sky

Curtained behind a combustible sky,
the morning rises and falls unnoticed,
consumed by smoke beneath
a gray stucco ceiling, so thick
its trowel marks protrude like claws
over the Tahoe Sierra—
once nature's Sistine Chapel.

The few remaining birds cower
bravely in prematurely emptied
nests cradled by the leafless
arms of penitent trees; yet
another migration interrupted.

As thirsty deer huddle together
near the undrinkable river, together,
our reflections perish in soot stained
water that soon will go dry again.

Lament

Cutting through the orchard
on autumn days like this

I imagine I hear them crying,
all those unpicked apples

left behind, filled with worms and tears,
their crispness lost as they too shrivel.

Others fret that they remain
uneaten, so small yet sweet,

cold flesh pained by
memories of the devoured.

How they wish to be ordinary.
Desired. Chosen.

But something went wrong.

Blemished and bruised,
they lie together yet alone.

Black-winged birds swarm above.
Yellow jackets buzz nearby, tempted.

Worms inch closer.
The unpicked yearn to be

seen as windfalls
given another chance.

Eight Points

Late autumn, the buck that has come to know me
paws at the rusted earth for what's still green

outside my window, unaware that I am present,
watching him rake his branching antlers—

chipped from generations of battle, like porcelain
consigned to a pawn shop shelf—

through piles of accumulated leaves and redwood duff.
Desperate to find acorns, as if something so small

      could feed winter's hunger.

      ::

We are old acquaintances, though I haven't seen him in a while.
Now, the dappled light from leafless trees grays his thinning fur.

I remember the time he popped my just-planted coastal redwood
out of the ground. The roots rose above us, briefly blocking out the

sky. I remember the time, body swollen with hormones, crazed by
the delicate scent of a doe, he charged me up a hill, where I slashed

at him with a brittle pine bough—old as bone—to wake him from
      his seasonal trance.

      ::

And now our eyes meet again, each afraid that the slightest move-
ment might disrupt our connection. What hurt me this time is his

shriveled right hindquarter, his awkward hobbling across the yard,
his raised white tail a flag of surrender, as if I were no longer

a threat. I used to try to make him into something he's not, some
metaphor for my own fading green, my rusting earth. But I know

he's just a tired old buck. And each of us are smelling the wood
smoke from last night's fires, both stinging and soothing us.

Together, so small under the same ashen sky.

When "If" Turns to "When"

Driving through a late August Gary Indiana,
the birthplace of the Jackson Five and U.S. Steel,
men in sleeveless undershirts over rolled-up
jeans and Red-Wing boots sweat like
Brando in "A Streetcar Named Desire."
They smoke on street corners, wait for something to happen.

Then snow begins to fall
like some heavenly offering.
I turn the wipers on and come to my senses,
sickened when I recognize
these swan-white flakes for what they are:
lead and benzene particulate matter
emitted from steel mill stacks.

One of the men starts dancing, not with joy.

::

Years later, on a midsummer night
we awaken. Coughing. Choking.

Wildfire Preparedness: purchase N95 respirators

"What we fear most, we call impossible, turn it into 'if.'"

The bedroom wallpapered
in thick bluish gray smoke and fear.
Inhaled air stings as we wheeze in terror

keep an air purifier in a safe room,

57

exhaling, our burnt breath hangs in the burnt air
pluming into images of death's
shadow against once bright walls.

"But it is only a wildfire in Yosemite
200 miles away, nothing to worry about."

Dreamers awakened by a fear no longer private.

Driven away from the safety of home

> *keep 100-foot hoses on each side of the house*

cars crawling behind cars crawling
like beetles that have lost their wings.
The white stuff falling the opposite of manna.

> *rake needles and leaves, clear brush near house*

Flocks of usually solitary geese and ducks
flee from an erased sky, then
huddle together on the pond.

They must be terrified too,

> *create defensible space, screen under deck areas*

curled in the dark flecks of ash stippling their feathers.

> *keep a go bag, have a plan*

"The ultimate fear being we will lose everything."

I can feel the warmth of the undertaker's hands.

"We take stock of all that we have,
not yet ready to let go,"

just a sign left in the window: *evacuated*.

There Is Nothing More Eloquent

than the terrifying silence of a golden eagle
gliding out of the tallest treetop, deep
into the shadows beneath the mountain.
Then dropping mouth first—a firefall.

::

Mallards. Jackrabbits. Bass below. Freeze.
Their world narrows. Fits inside the eagles'
outline. Everything caught in his shadow
waits until he stalls midair.
Their intricate shapes like paper cutouts
or target range pin-ups.
Eventually, he'll grip his victim
and drag it back up into the heavens.

::

But there are not always predators here,
I tell my son. And not always prey.
Carrying their memories and trash
back home, the tourists follow
these narrow dirt roads that break
away from the mountain like rivers
leaving their source. And the birds, too. Return.

Velvet

Thrashing in the shadows of a timber cut,
tearing bloody strips of velvet
from your branching head ornament,

your warm blood froths, splatters about
your mantle, muscling against last year's sapling.

Such lathered movements:
a memorial of brutal passion

deep within the forest, the dry brush
cracking, a curl of black dust rising
round reddened antlers.

Panting, gasping, exhausted, you pause
to stomp on jostled sticks,

before roaring back to attack, as if
possessed, to scrape the velvet away
from those prized antlers.

Such dedicated effort to shed former layers.
To wrestle free from the grasp of the old.

Sea Lion

The gulls hover, patient as a midwife.
Other birds perched at the edge of the hedgerow
pace anxiously, hungry for new life.

The surf continues its
opening and closing
beckoning and sending away

while she lies broadside to a sea
washing over and cleansing her.
Her sand-speckled fur glows in

the unbroken sunlight. Guttural
coughs. Body trembling. Without
warning, blood seeps like red ink

into soft sand, and the squirming pup
nudged by its mother toward the open
sea opens its throat to wail. To sing.

And the gulls swoop in to feast on what remains.

Striped reef fish glide past
an impossibly colored canvas—
not from painters' brush

Bottomless Water

The boat has nearly capsized, its keel
reaching desperately for air. Though

sunburned we're white with fear, leaning
as far over the upper rail as we can without falling,

hoping our weight can save us.
We make every effort to re-center

our greatest fear: being exposed to
something we have no control over.

We work to persuade ourselves
we can prevent *it* by doing the right thing.

We do not know how the story will end.
At the moment it has lost its narrative.

The water that was to hold us up has not.
As we move through it, we realize we are

shapeless as the sea all around us.

Puzzle Pieces

Early morning rain has
released its leaves from

the stand of maple beside the house.

They land like puzzle pieces
fitting perfectly in place,

their tips tenderly touching.
When the day again turns dry

the leaves will crumble beneath
the feet of children—dancing, fleeing.

They leave brief, henna-hued stains
on the sidewalk before gradually

washing away.

A Second Look

A twilight walk, fresh forest snow, silence.
Our boot-crunch on the ice crystals
alerts a field mouse to take cover.

The cold air makes our words visible
as the conversation grows darker
against the whiteness: letters on a page.

Briefly, they curl back to us—
then vanish as we watch, grateful.

Beyond the Field

You see them on lawns and in sidewalk cracks
sometimes covering an entire field,
their thickheaded yellow flowers
a delicate display of color

maturing at the end of summer into
fuzzy white globes ready to
lift off and circumnavigate the earth
their seeds parachute back to us,

                    forgiving.

Pick another. Blow lightly. Watch
the puff expand. Drift in the breeze.
Float beyond the field.
And beyond that another field.

Cuttings, Mid-September Morning

Late summer turning   to early fall, several
nights of frost lace   the garden. Things
we have come to know   ending.

Outside the florists shop   I press my nose
against the glass   for one last   glimpse.
Inside,   the room   colored from leaves
on yesterday's   cut branches   refract

light against the walls   —a green that seems
to burst into itself,   washing the walls in hues
soft to the touch as a newborn's lanugo
what the florist calls   *"light fall."*

::

Her shears   *click and*
snip delicate tips.   She shapes and sculpts,
fashions and fettles, pinching   black discolored,

mostly dead,   leaves from sprigs of Black
Oak, Silver Maple, Coffee Berry,   later
to be gathered   in bunches, or bouquets,

wrapped in paper to form a cone,   after
the death   arranged in a clear glass vase
to make room for   tomorrow's vibrant cuttings.

Cultivation

You might stop to watch a tractor
tilling flattened fields from end to end
turning back on itself, its gears grinding
a melancholic drone of autumn

as churning plow blades buckle half-baked soil
trailed by swirling dust and raucous blackbirds
fighting over swollen melons left to rot,
preying on worms and squirming bugs.

The furrows of our fallow minds
are filled with old grievances still
to be worked over. False accusations,
disappointments, slights, family gripes

until plowed under, their corrupting stench
miscoloring the best poems of spring
with black rot, hunger, so much longing

pushing their way to the surface,
like star thistle and bindweed
nourished by last season's decay.

Tending the Forest

Someone has been tending the forest.
In my absence a maze of tidy piles

appeared along my woodland trail
the way mushrooms pop-up after
fall's first shower.

Trees topped, their branches
forming unlit pyres,
arched boughs set atop the piles:

the forest pattern rearranged.

The woodsman shaped the contours
like Ojibwe homes:

a hundred small abodes
now spot the woodland floor.

Through thinned branches
distressed light dapples the forest.

Something is gone
from this place

where I once gathered
and held what I believed

to be mine.

Reading Our Limbed Monterey Pine

A clearness returns to me.
When I finally slow down
and look long enough
at such an unruffled morning,
wordless faces in the trees

that once knew my name
as I assumed I knew theirs.

Wrinkled with folds of time.
Topped with lichen coppered
like museum name plates.
Stacked head upon head
upon trunk carved like totems.
Eyelids heavy with wisdom.

Spikes of sunlight steam
the coastal fog. No ocean left
out there. Just some delicate
magenta rhododendron petals

clustered in the same moist soil
as other bodies. And I think, too late,
I recognize you now. Clearly. Shrouded
in new life. In the lacey green filigree of bracken.

In the two tiny birds ascending
and returning. In the ocean I know
is out there, somewhere, still.

Final Accomplishment

While mountain peaks reflect
their true faces across a smooth lake surface,
their ragged borders bleed
into the margins. Watercolors
staining where page meets water.

Kokanee salmon assemble in the shallows
to lay their eggs. Unborn mirrors
of themselves. Skin as red as the
violently beautiful sun above.
As leaves before they rust and wither.

Such firm flesh softens, yields to
their inevitable benediction. And life.

¤

The Noises of Night

¤

The trees' growth rings
reveal more than its size
only after death

The Noises of Night

The melody of darkness
has softened the day
into cradle songs

this rhythmic basso of distant subways
talking back and forth
muffled groans of switch engines clearing tracks

the moan of low-flying planes
vibrating copper gutters
softly rattling windowpanes.

All this, a lullaby now
to half-closed eyes
still cherishing those

shards of dreams
that cannot soften
the absence of

lost childhood.

Mississippi

My mother often broke in
when my sister and I practiced our spelling
rising from her chair and standing
tall as the four i's in Mississippi
chiming: *M-i-s-s-i-s-s-i-p-p-i*
throwing herself into each letter

E-n-u-n-c-i-a-t-i-n-g
measuring out letters like gin in a cocktail glass.
And maybe this *was* her tonic
this affectation born of frustration
at leaving school early to help keep the family farm
while longing still to be the last one standing
at the spring spelling bee.

::

One summer afternoon I caught my mother
at the kitchen table, a Kool dangling from her bony fingers
imitating the gestures of sophisticated women
the smoke wreathing up and over the Magic Chef
in the shape of the S's in Mississippi.
Seeing me, she doused the cigarette

and tried to slip it back into the pack
next to the others their fine tobacco rolled
tightly, sheathed in smooth white paper
perfumed with a touch of menthol
and filtered to hold the tar and breath.

::

Later I stole a couple
hidden in the kitchen cupboard behind the sugar
and pedaled to the East River cattails
to a spot in the shadows of the trestle
close enough to the hobo encampment
to smell wood-fire-canned beans
and creosote from Chicago Northwestern
cross-ties baking in late August heat.

Lighting the smoke, I was surprised
at the way my hand trembled
at the sulfur burn in my nose, the acrid taste.
How I could feel my mother's desperation,
the glowing orange tip turning to gray ash
dropping onto my sweatshirt,
burning a jagged hole. Our smoke
curling back slowly to the river and disappearing.

My Father's Last Year

I came upon the trout
sunning itself in the shallows
of a mountain lake,
both of us surprised
at our solitudes being interrupted.

With a flap of a tail, it twisted from view,
dropping into a deep place beyond sunlight.

Later, memories surfaced like bubbles, breath:
my mostly silent father spitting into the lake
for good luck before his first cast,
cutting ten-pound test line with his teeth,
squinting while threading the leader
through the hook's eye with thickened fingers.

Muttering to himself in the late afternoon light,
he revealed a softness. By joining two
lines with the patience of a seamstress,
he taught me how best to tie
an enduring blood knot.

Singer

Those afternoons were like no others
the two of us working, my mother's
stockings rolled around her ankles

the room filled with muffled clicks
scissors closing on old socks
snipping them into strips

the Singer whining as it resisted
through gritted teeth my mother coaxing it along

sometimes whistling to the machine's hum
tapping her foot to the floor-pedal
consulting me about color schemes
her fingers over mine needling

cloth that often bunched and she
taught me how to best smooth things out
caressing the old buzzing machine

scripted with gold filigree
its overloaded needle bar unable to rest
until the job was done

she had a feel for the design of things—
brightening the browns with argyle reds and purples
as she stitched the pieces together

matching sock colors to her imagined pattern
creating a threadbare masterpiece
that might just last forever

Mother Poems

I. Hymnal

I stood on the squat stool
about as tall as you, mother,
the two of us at the kitchen sink
finishing up the dinner dishes
your hands in the dishpan
washing, rinsing, handing the plates
over for me to dry with flour sacks
you'd hemmed into dishtowels,
for a moment each of us gripping
the same plate the way we held the hymnal
singing together at Sunday mass.

II. Wool Socks

On days I stayed home from school with the flu
tucked in bed by hands that mothered six of us
mostly boys, I'd often wake to smell onions
boiling, hear you heating the pot tending
your cure for my congestion.

What I remember most is not
the way you bent over me, placing
the onions in a yellowed athletic
sock you'd scissored with a surgeon's skill to fit

my chest but the barely audible click
of safety pins you plucked one by one from
your lips and opened to secure the healing
sock to my pajama top.

III. Wash Water

Later, your fingers in my palms
like the delicate legs of small birds.

Surprised by their continued warmth,
their smoothness, the reflective sheen of age.

Until I can no longer hold it, I keep
your hands in mine. Never too tightly.

The way I cup warm morning wash water,
sometimes seeing myself on its surface.

I splash my face one last time
before you trickle away.

Three Mornings

You awaken the morning after
to a few edible kernels
lost in a dish of peanut shells,
the debris not yet
sifted through
for what might remain.
For just a taste of sustenance.

::

You awaken to amber coals
still lit beneath fireplace ash,
evening logs
once thick as a man's skull
now smoldering, covered
by a fluff of gray down.
You stir them with a poker.

::

You awaken to remnants of a family quarrel.
Unslept-in beds. Chipped porcelain. A lingering
scent of smoke. The house
gone numb. Anger
boiling over with collected
grievances. Three generations
awaiting the balm of a conversation
that too will turn to ash.

Swallow

She sits so upright, as if in a straitjacket,
in the old highchair that still wears her grand-

mother's stains and scratches, feeding herself
blueberries for the first time. Glowing from within,

not yet dimmed by the world, she swells
her cheeks like bruises and removes my hand

from hers, finally gripping the spoon without
help. Her open palm like a phantom stop

sign extends out toward the kind of father
she no longer needs.

Caesura

We take comfort in patterns

the repetition of squares in a quilt
the segments of a ram's horn curl
the winged seed tips of a dried pinecone

all these blank spaces made fuller

now there's room for us to see ourselves
in the repeated measures of a body's melody

although we think it's what's there
that holds meaning, is it really

the pauses that sustain us

the breach in the incoming tide
the break in a bird's song

the gap between toes of a cloven hoof
the white space that surrounds this poem

the hesitation in your voice when
you whisper my name in the dark

the enduring absence of that final goodbye

Missing My Daughter

Barren branches frame what I want to forget,
their tips now a pattern of dots I struggle to reconnect

against the sky's dark canvas.
I ache for the leaves' fluctuating moods,

that summer hue that flares
red and ochre in October, paper

dresses dropped then buried beneath the snow.
A brightly feathered bird, tiny,

has found a safe spot to land
in my empty branches. I look away for a moment,

and when I look back the bird is gone.

Patient deer prune ivy
choking our last tree trunk—
reveals hidden textures

Cathedral

Our canoe slips downstream with the darkness
over a stretch of the Snake that rises
in western Wyoming. The Grand Tetons
steepling above us, a cathedral.

The cold aluminum paddle stiff in my hand
parts the water with each blistered stroke.
We row like sinners who have come here
to struggle with death, borne along by fomented waters

hurtling our delicate vessel
down the river's broad gullet.
We grind bony whitewater rapids,
throats dry as a rusted pipe organ.

Wagner's thunderclaps ring in my head.
We crescendo into the suddenly calm backwater.

I remove the clear, Zip Lock bag holding her ashes
from my unbuttoned shirt pocket,
the last hours of daylight slipping away,

10,000 years of life empty into the water
blossoming into shapes: a hand opening
and closing in slow motion, the swish of
a trout's tail fin treading water,
a woman's long hair blown back in the wind,

a bird about to take to the sky.

Things That Don't Change

You find the cutoff, he told me,
by noticing things that don't change—
somewhere between two distant pines,
gnarled and bent, over 400 years old.

Navigating the landscape by angles and curves,
coordinates pass through your body,
waypoints mapped between heart and head.

Booting it to the top as the crow flies,
we leave the ice-scoured valley for thinning forests
treading on dried peat and bog, slowing only
to traverse waist-high Manzanita, scrambling
over boulders, sliding on talus and scree.

We take a break; he asks how I am doing,
grabs a stick, scrapes a line in the earth
showing me our path. And I let it all in

as my buried father awakens and gently calls
to me from the jumble of Manzanita shadows,
from the brown horsefly strafing my forehead.

The buff-bellied marmot chattering his teeth
revives a memory of my father's razor clearing
the world from his face. The dry mountain sage
of his aftershave. The same crunches and breaks
of pine needles as his late-night footsteps on the hard-
wood floor at home, trying so hard not to disturb

those things in us he prayed would never change.

Wolf at the Door

His chilled hands folded, a crucifix on his chest,
a still life framed in black and white,
a boxed gift nested in tissue paper.

At the funeral home, sad figures murmur
patting one another on the back
tenderly, the way we soothe children,
gripping each other's hands, reluctant to let go.

Then moving slowly on to the next mourner
as if underwater,
in no hurry to say good-bye.

Or maybe it's more like a wicker picnic basket,
half-hinged lid folded-open
to uncover half the truth about life and death
red-checkered gingham replacing the fine
white satin, the wolf at the door turned back.

Next morning these practiced knots no longer hold.
Tossing and turning, cursing
the animal sounds on the roof above me,
too much like shovels digging my own grave,
white cotton sheets already turned down to my waist,
I lie naked and reluctant below.

Selkie

Bitter cold, low December sun,
a briny chill from Monterey Bay—me
standing on the west-facing promenade,
gripping the iron railing for dear life,
fighting thoughts of losing my partner.

Swift-winged gulls surf the breeze,
peering down at me, shivering,

shifting my weight foot to foot,
trying to balance myself against
the cold earth, contemplating sea
otters suspended on an uncalm surface.
In the dark wetness of thick fur, intent,
they work abalone shells back and forth
in tiny hands, assured, as if attempting to
solve some greater mystery.

Others are holding hands to not drift
this far away from each other, themselves.

And there is something else, an object,
a person, a woman, naked, moving like
a Celtic step dancer between the otters,
kelp tangled in her silver hair, ponytail
swinging like a metronome keeping
track of future losses. As if nothing
could be easier. In this place where no
human could survive for long, she is
one with the sea, with the myth I've
gifted her.

Returning to solid earth, she sheds the
cold skin of night, gone naked all around us.

Swallowing the Light

Body wrapped in her favorite blanket, whimpering
in my arms, I stumble down the staircase to the car.

Plant her across the children's laps in the back seat.
Recognize the brokenness in their young faces

as they whisper *hush little baby don't you cry*,
knowing she can only listen. Trembling, her eyes

wan and rheumy, our hearts hanging like an off-season
pinata. Driving down Christmas Eve streets

that should belong to a few men bloated with
the season dressed up like Santa. At the vet

we ring the doorbell and wait. Wait. Lit by
flashing red neon lights from the tattoo

shop next door. Fog thick as gauze, merciless,
swallowing the light. The red. The red light in her eyes.

Someone opens the door, and we hand her over.
A siren wails down a neighboring street. Help on the way.

Someone else brought back to life. As we leave
to go home, empty handed, still wrapped in that trembling.

The Scent of Citrus

In long shadows and chestnut-scented air,
my mother pulls marigolds and zinnias,

repeating *come on now, come on now* through gritted teeth.
Her harvest overwintered in the cellar. Dried plants

twined to the rafters by their roots above Kerr canning jars
bursting with preserves and wooden bushel baskets seeping

savory red, yellow, and green apples nestled with rutabagas,
russet potatoes and carrots cellared to hold tight their sweetness.

Her gentle touch converts sunlight and raw earth
into flowers and sustenance for the family.

At bedtime, dishes in their place, counter wiped clean,
all the day's garbage swaddled in newspaper, deposited

in the breezeway can, metal cover clicked tight
against nighttime visitors, she comes to tuck me in.

She smooths the quilt with an open hand. My head peeks
out from beneath a neatly folded sheet. The scent of citrus lingers

on her paper-thin lips. So many oranges she peels and quarters
every evening to get her vitamin C. She bends over to kiss

the top of my head, sealing a note in an envelope
waiting to be sent off unread into the night.

Looking for the House with the Body

Half-past three, I sit up in bed cursing
diesels hissing up my hill, whining before

air brakes squeal like a pig in a butcher shop.
A two-ton brick-red truck shakes

the house like a temblor, stops.
A uniformed man steps out and moves

swiftly amidst blue and red lights flashing.
A spotlight ricochets off porch windows

like the nickel machines at the Ocean Beach Penny Arcade
gathering such intensity you'd think someone

had won the jackpot. "They're coming here next,"
I warn her. "I've heard them before at the Brodys

and the Andersons." "I only hear them when you do,"
she says. "Yes, I say, yes. They're at the Smith's place."

"It won't be long now," she says,
reaching for my hand in the dark

as the men outside keep searching for the body.
"Yes," I say, knowing what she means. "Not long."

Cadaver Lab

Not the stainless-steel walls
or the bodies reclining on gleaming tables,
hands, faces and genitals hidden
the way children cover the privates of dolls
with ill-fitting, mismatched clothes.

Not brains kept in old one-gallon
ice cream tubs with brightly colored
lids and plastic handles.

Not skin hardened to pachyderm brown
wrinkles dried in folds
organs floating in styrene vats
to mix and match for study.
Delicate flesh damaged by hundreds
of incisions made by anatomy students.

Not even the excess fat scraped
and dumped into steel containers
for disposal at day's end.

Nor the incessant humming of ventilation fans
carrying away fixative fumes
along with nausea from empty stomachs.

Not the litanies of respect for the cadavers
and their families for their gift to science.
Not the cracked skin surfaces kept moist by spritzing.

No. What I can't forget: the remains
of multi-colored wires, copper ends frayed,
pacemakers long gone

lest someone get shocked by the dead.
Breast inserts leaking silicon,
steel hips and plastic knees.

The tattered flaps of tattooed skin
one stained bluish-green
inscribed with a tribal circle of life.

All that remains
after our souls are gone.

The Beauty in Letting Go

Now only the thin pine frame hangs on the bedroom wall
unburdened of accumulated grief

and the irreconcilable weight of a photograph
removed this morning, its colors long faded

worked on for years by gleaming-sunlight
and the gloom of gray days

reflected off the double casement glass
it faced on the opposite wall.

Sounds of bickering, second guessing, betrayals
and damage are gone, like leaves dropped

from a tree, revealing open space inside the frame
intact corners holding

the brightness and burden of possibility.
In the darkness, reds and blues regain their original hues.

The beauty in letting go mingles
 with knowing we cannot know

what lies anew within the frame.
While everywhere sunflowers sprout buds

as promised, and days grow longer,
the lake water flattens.

There is an evenness to moods—
still, we cannot tell what happiness we might find.

About the Author

John Schneider lives and works in Berkeley, California. His work has been published in *The Worcester Review, Tampa Review,The Inflectioinist Review, The American Journal of Poetry, California Fire and Water: A Climate Crisis Anthology,* and elsewhere. His poetry has been a Merit Award winner in the *Atlanta Review* 2021 International Poetry Competition He is also a two-time Pushcart Prize nominee.

Made in the USA
Monee, IL
03 December 2022

19496257R00056